An Ellis Island Story— The Cinabros, A Recollection

Robert H. Cinabro

To GINA!,
CON PIACERE!

VANTAGE PRESS
New York

Excerpts from *The Battle for Rome,* by Robert Katz, copyright © 2003, Simon & Schuster, New York, are reprinted with permission.

Cover design by Susan Thomas

FIRST EDITION

Copyright © 2005 by Robert H. Cinabro

Published by Vantage Press, Inc.
419 Park Ave. South, New York, NY 10016

Manufactured in the United States of America
ISBN: 0-533-14935-5

Library of Congress Catalog Card No.: 2004093184

0 9 8 7 6 5 4 3 2 1

To the memories of my father and mother,
Louis and Maria

Contents

Preface

2003 marked one hundred years since Antonio Cinabro at age twenty-two all alone boarded the steamship *Phoenicia* in Naples, Italy, for the long voyage to America. It is the beginning of the Cinabro family story in America. I never knew him, as he died long before I was born. The centennial of the arrival of the family in America is but one reason I chose to write this. In addition, the Ellis Island records now available motivated me to uncover previously unknown aspects of the story. Most importantly, the aging and passing of loved ones inspired me to capture much of the history as told to me before these stories are lost forever.

I want to emphasize that this is not a genealogical history of the Cinabros or Breviglieris. It does not trace the history before my grandparents, which I hope someday my children or their children will be motivated to explore. With a few exceptions this is a record of my immediate lineage, focused on my mother and father. My aunts and uncles deserve their own histories, but I have made an exception for Aunt Antoinette, who because of her central role in my life and the life of the family has been given some special mention. I apologize if I have unintentionally offended anyone by not including mention of their names or stories.

This is the truth as I know it, based on what was told to me and what I have read and seen. I have not embellished these stories, because they need no embellishment.

Any mistakes or inaccuracies are unintentional. I will have succeeded with this if some day, someone of my posterity reads this, and just for a time remembers these people who lived, loved, fought, and survived so long ago. Maybe someone will be inspired to visit the first house in Blue Island, or Culver, or the Guggenheim Museum in Venice, or the site in Via Rasella in Rome, or, of course, Ellis Island. If so, this will have been worth it.

Finally, I hope my children and grandchildren will learn of the Eschenburgs and Harlands. They are the other half of the story.

Acknowledgments

I want to everlastingly thank my beloved late mother, Maria Breviglieri Cinabro, for giving me the benefit of learning of her wartime years by recollecting and telling me the stories as I grew up, especially the story of the Via Rasella incident in Rome, and of her escapes from death during the war. She fostered the interest and curiosity with me, which will remain long after her death. My dear Aunt, Junior, or Antoinette, or "Dorothy" was a very influential and dominant force in my life, from my earliest childhood, through law school and into adulthood. I owe her so much, especially the stories of the Cinabro family and the early years. Through their oral histories both women have contributed so much to this story.

I could not have written of the Culver years of my late father Louis without the kindness and help of Historian and Archivist Bob Hartman of the Culver Academies, who took time out of his busy schedule to meet with me in September of 2003 and to allow me to use and copy my father's file. Mr. Hartman is a fine, dedicated person and a noteworthy representative of that proud school at Culver.

A source that I used a lot during the writing of the Rome war years was the book *The Battle for Rome,* written by Robert Katz and published by Simon & Schuster in 2003. His kind permission was granted for quoting and paraphrasing from that wonderful and overdue book, and I thank him very much.

The Ellis Island records and the American Family

Immigration History Center archives and website regarding Ellis Island were an invaluable tool to tracing Antonio's saga through Ellis Island, as well as the subsequent trip by the family in 1921.

Finally, a special thanks to my son, Michael Thomas Cinabro, for his help with the computer, which was of great assistance to making this an easier project than it might have been.

1

A Beginning: Ellis Island 1903, Antonio Cinabro

The steamship S.S. *Phoenicia* set sail from Naples, Italy, on February 21, 1903. It arrived in New York Harbor on March 16, 1903. The twenty-three days on the North Atlantic in the winter could only have been rough, freezing and choppy for those on board. Arriving at Ellis Island along with a large number of other immigrants was twenty-two-year-old Antonio (Anthony) Cinabro. He was apparently in good health when he arrived. He came from Muro Lucano, in Southern Italy, in a hilly, remote region of small towns and poverty. The area is known as Basilicata. He could not read or write according to the ship's manifest, but whether this is true is unclear. Education was something that he probably learned by facing life and not the classroom. He was already a trained and skilled shoemaker and played the clarinet. Even if it is assumed he had some form of secondary education, he did not attend a college or university.

The hometown of the Cinabros, Muro Lucano (literally translated "Lucano Wall"), is located in a region of Italy described as recently as 1996 as being "remote and wild." (Dorling Kindersley Travel Guides, Italy, 1996, page 499). The town is the site of an ancient village known as Numistri, and it was the scene of an important ancient battle between the Romans and the Cathaginians under Hannibal in the Second Punic War. Basilicata is located in the foot area of the boot of Italy, and Muro Lucano is not far from Potenza, which is the provincial capital. There is a renowned cathedral in the town, and the town itself is a diocese seat. The countryside is rugged and hilly, and houses are crammed together in small towns in the region, almost sitting on rocks and cliffs. There are a lot of Greek ruins in the area, and the topography is stunningly beautiful and scenic. But poverty was rampant in the early part of the twentieth century, and much of the population emigrated to North and South America, leaving a sparsely populated region. One must assume that life in Muro Lucano in 1903 was provincial, rough, dominated by tradition, and beset by poverty and superstition. America must have seemed like another planet.

Antonio was married, but in 1903 they had no children. It is unclear why he left his wife Rosemary in Italy but economic uncertainty and the risk of settling in a new country must have played a part in their decision to let Antonio arrive first. It is likely, according to the manifest, that he only had $6.00 in his possession when he arrived in America. There is no evidence that he did anything but go directly to the Chicago area, probably riding a train in coach from New York, and settle in the suburban railroad town of Blue Island, directly south of Chicago. He took up his trade of shoemaking, and was later joined by his wife, Rosemary (Pacella), whom he had married before 1903. According to the Ellis Island records, Rosemary arrived at Ellis Island on November 26, 1906, more than three years after Antonio, on the ship the *Florida*, having set sail from Naples. She was twenty-seven years of age when she arrived.

The earliest picture in 1907 shows a slim, distinguished looking, well-dressed man with a mustache, beside his wife in a Victorian dress. Despite the economic challenges he and the family would always face, being dressed fashionably well was always evident. They both obviously had pride and dignity.

What brought Antonio to Blue Island is unclear, though there is some indication a friend from Muro Lucano had settled there earlier. The ship's manifest suggests a relative may have been living in Chicago, but it is more likely that a friend by the name of Guiseppe (Joe) Chieppa had encouraged Antonio to emigrate.

One can only imagine whether he had second thoughts as he made the voyage across the Atlantic in a four-masted old steamship, probably travelling in steerage or third class, leaving a sunny and familiar environment to face a world completely alien and unknown. The food must have been plain, the sleeping conditions crowded and poor at best. This was not a pleasure cruise, and there were no floor shows, cruise directors or multi-course meals. He probably ate his meals below deck at a common table with many other people, and the fare was probably the same every day and simple. The temperatures must have been unbearable. He would have to face a lot of icy, windy and damp winters in Chicago, but nothing could have compared to the frigid, wind blown decks of the *Pheonicia*. It undeniably took an act of courage to make this trip. The North Atlantic, which is rough even in the summer, was even worse in February.

Though family members would cross the Atlantic again many times, this trip was the hardest, and most significant, of all. He would return to Italy in time for World War I, but he would never be anything but American. He was part of the great wave of Italian immigration at this time of American history, and he was part of what

3

became the Ellis Island story. His name is now on the wall of honor at Ellis Island. He would go through Ellis Island a second time, in 1921, after having returned to Italy, and experiencing the war and military service, but he never would leave America's shores after that.

He would be known as Tony in America. He was by all accounts a good and kindly man. He was generous to a fault, honest, hard working, and never in trouble with the law. At a time when the Mafia and "The Black Hand" preyed upon the often-discriminated against Italian immigrants who came to the shores of America, and offered temptations and protections which the established law enforcement agencies could not or would not do, he never gave in to these pressures.

2

The *Phoenicia*

The steamship which brought Antonio Cinabro to the New World was named after the ancient civilization of traders and navigators which flourished in the Middle East about 1000 B.C. It had one stack and four masts and looked very much nineteenth century. It was built in Hamburg, Germany, in 1894. It was 450 feet long and could carry 2060 passengers. It displaced 7,155 gross tons and could do thirteen knots. It was sold to the Russian navy in 1904, only one year after Antonio arrived at Ellis Island. It was eventually scrapped in 1937 as the war clouds were engulfing Europe. One can only say that it must have been extremely crowded on the *Phoenicia* when Antonio traveled the more than three weeks to America. The amenities had to have been few indeed, and the lack of stabilizers must have made a lot of people sick during the voyage. There are no known descriptions of this trip he made, and if the manifest is to be believed, maybe it is because he could not write, but this is uncertain.

The *Phoenicia*

Antonio and Rosemary—1907

3

The Early Years, Blue Island, and Back to Italy

Blue Island, Illinois, is and was a railroad town. The sounds of the train whistles moaning in the middle of the night became familiar to the Cinabros. In this working-class town of Italian and German and other immigrants the Cinabro family took root. There is little record of the early years. They must have rented a small apartment, probably a flat in a house. It is certain that Antonio began his trade as a shoemaker and shoe repairman. Rosemary tended to the home and hearth, and there is no record that she ever worked outside the home. Antonio's knowledge of the clarinet enabled him to play as a skilled musician in bands when he was not working his trade. On September 18, 1907, the firstborn child, Louis, arrived in the family. There would be a total of eight births, with one stillborn child. Six children would live to maturity. The seventh, Filomena, would die after three months, in 1923.

Louis was followed by Arthur, and then Maria Antoinette (also nicknamed Dorothy but always called Antoinette), Morris (Maurice), Armand, and Henry in 1922. Filomena the last born child in 1923 would be the first to die. Antoinette, Maurice and Armand would be born in Italy, and Louis, Arthur and Henry would be born in America.

Sometime after 1909 Rosemary, Louis and Arthur,

travelled to Italy, and went back to Muro Lucano, with Antonio following later. The reasons for the return to Italy are not clear. Rosemary may have felt lonely and a longing for her native land, and economics may have played a part. Additionally, she had inherited a house in Muro which Antoinette recalled had three rooms and a balcony. Antonio worked at his trade of shoemaking in Muro, and the Cinabros remained in Italy until 1921. They then returned to America. First Antonio returned with Arthur, and then Rosemary returned with Louis, Antoinette, Armand and Maurice. The date of arrival in Ellis Island for Rosemary and the children (her second trip through Ellis Island) was May 18, 1921. The port of departure was again Naples. The ship was the *Duca d' Aosta,* a much more modern looking ship than the *Phoenicia,* with two stacks and a passenger capacity of 1836. Antoinette remembered playing as a little girl with ball games on the deck. This trip in May across the Atlantic must surely have been much more pleasant than the solo voyage in 1903 of Antonio.

But before their return to America in 1921 war came to Italy in 1914, as it did to most of Europe, and Antonio and the family spent all of World War I in Italy. Antonio honorably served as a sergeant in the Italian Army in World War I. The dates of service and details have not been discovered. Photos show Antonio with an army unit in the town of Bari, in the south of Italy, in 1916. He may have been a medic, but this is not certain. He obviously felt patriotic and still enough of an Italian to serve in the army. There is no documentation about the details of his discharge from the army. The war ended in 1918, and thereafter soon the Cinabros decided to go back to Blue Island.

Following the family's second voyage through Ellis

Island in 1921, Rosemary and Antonio would remain for all their lives in Blue Island. Antonio would travel and play his clarinet and sometimes the saxophone in bands, sometimes leaving for the events outside of Chicago. The main source of income for the growing family was the trade of Antonio as a shoemaker. He eventually had his own little store, where he was a sole proprietor. He would work six days a week, with Saturday being the busiest day. He never owned or drove an automobile, and never took a vacation.

As an Italian small businessman, he became the subject of at least one attempt at extortion by what was known as "The Black Hand." "The Black Hand" was not truly the Mafia, but was a loosely organized group of extortionists who preyed on small tradesmen and businesses, making threats with notes delivered anonymously, and if money was paid nothing bad would happen to the store or the owner or the family. This form of extortion in the 1910s and 1920s was common, and was probably copied by individuals and various groups. Antonio must have been a ripe target, being a newly arrived immigrant. It was related to me that he withstood at least one such extortion attempt, and kept his business and integrity (and life!) intact.

Rosemary was an accomplished cook, and took care of the children. In an era when women (if they worked at all) were only teachers or nurses. Rosemary was an Old World example of the matriarch of the family. Her macaroni with tomato sauce was her specialty. She was strict, old-fashioned, and devoted to the family's above all. She would rise early, tend to the family daily routine, and make sure all the meals were ready on time. Washing clothes from an old scrubbing board, ironing, patching torn clothing, and cleaning house were all part of a strict regimen. Raising six children was for her all the work she needed. She often spoke in a Southern Italian dialect.

Loneliness must have visited her when Antonio travelled, and the strange ways of the new world and culture were difficult to adapt to. After they returned to America in 1921 the family lived for a time in a rented flat in a house in Blue Island near Vermont Street. From there they moved to the first house they owned on Western Avenue, on the south side of Blue Island.

4

Louis Cinabro

The first-born of Antonio and Rosemary was Louis, born on September 18, 1907. The first pictures show him with a traditional long Christening gown in the Old World way. His early years were spent in Blue Island, but at around age two or three he travelled back to Muro Lucano with Rosemary and Arthur. When he returned to America he was fourteen years of age, arriving through Ellis Island in 1921 on the *Duca d'Aosta*. A picture taken in 1914 shows him and Arthur in Italy, dressed very much in the way of Southern Italians at the time. After coming back to America he would spend the next few years attending school. He attended the Lincoln and Seymour schools in Blue Island. From there he went to high school, graduating as class valedictorian in 1928 at Blue Island High School. Though small in stature, he was on the high school football team as a reserve quarterback. He took a scientific course in high school, and had aspirations to go to medical school.

He entered the University of Chicago, graduating with a Bachelor's degree in Philosophy in 1932. It is believed he may have been the first of the family to graduate from a college or university. He loved foreign languages, and would major in this field, becoming proficient in his lifetime in five languages: Spanish, French, Italian, German, and Portuguese. The Romance languages would be his forte. He also studied science in college, and began medical school upon graduation.

After one year in medical school at the University of Chicago, he left the scientific field. He always had a greater love of the language arts, and he subsequently took graduate courses at the University of Chicago in languages. He was most comfortable in literary disciplines. The beginning of the Great Depression following the stock market crash of 1929 made it very difficult to get jobs, even for a college-educated person. Louis would recall that anti-Italian discrimination also played an insidious role. There were jobs that were simply not available to those whose names ended in a vowel, as he used to say. The Italians still had not assimilated in American society.

There were several influences on Louis that would always dominate his life. The first was classical music, undoubtedly helped by the fact that Antonio (now always known as Tony) played in a band. Italian opera was in vogue, especially through the stardom of the great Italian tenor Enrico Caruso. The operas of Verdi and Puccini were always played on the phonograph. The second, and most pervasive influence on his life, was literature and reading. A voracious reader all his life, he was especially fond of Russian literature, and the great Russian masters Tolstoy and Dostoyevski. He also read widely in French, Italian, and of the English classical authors and poets such as Dickens, Byron, Keats and Shelley. Books were always present wherever Louis lived, and even war or the Great Depression could not deter him from reading.

Louis loved to write, and to be a playwright would be his dream at any early age. Evidence of at least five plays written by Louis have survived. Two were copyrighted in

2003. Apparently one play was performed briefly at the Masonic Temple in Blue Island.

At the age of twenty-three, while in college, Louis wrote an article for a national publication from New York called, *Il Calzolaio* (The Shoemaker). Louis discusses and analyzes the shoemaker class and its future in American economic and social life. The article evinces his wide vocabulary and writing skills, but also his implicit admiration for his father's craft and trade, and it is obvious he respected his father. As Antoinette put it, as close as he was to his father, Louis adored his mother. His mother would be a dominant influence, and his home in Blue Island would always be dear to him. He would return many times to his hometown, and not even war nor long distance could keep him from thinking about it and writing about it. He was proud to be an American, and he was proud to be from Blue Island, and, by extension, Chicago.

The arts and literature would be his passion, and education was his watchword. Though the future would compel him to face war, travel, adversity and economic challenges, circumstances never kept him apart from his beloved books. He could read five books at one time and could devour them easily in a week or less. He could be reading one book in French, one in Italian and one in English in the same day. Until his seventies he would read widely and deeply. His life was always marked by intellectual curiosity and a profound respect for education.

Louis came of age in Blue Island during the "Roaring Twenties." He was age fourteen when he arrived back in America from Muro Lucano, and the formative years of his life in high school and college were dominated by prohibition, news of Al Capone, the newspaper stories of Chicago gangland activities of bootlegging and murder, and such events as "The St. Valentine's Day Massacre." The economy during the 1920s was relatively good, and education was available to Louis, though not a life of luxury or spoils. Blue Island was a site for one of Al Capone's "roadhouses," the Burr Oak Hotel, and Louis and his brothers must have learned and read about the nefarious activities of these places. Besides the career of Al Capone, famous crimes in Chicago such as the Loeb and Leopold case involving the murder of an innocent child by the name of Bobby Franks dominated the headlines, and Louis would always recount these stories. He keenly followed current events, became very knowledgeable about the crime history of Blue Island and South Cook County, and he attended as a curious citizen the wedding of the sister of Al Capone, Mafalda Capone, to John Maritote. The wedding had been announced in the Chicago newspapers, and all citizens were invited to attend. He would be in a large crowd watching from outside the church, and he saw the famed brother of Al Capone, Ralph (known in the media as "Bottles") Capone.

Louis read newspapers eagerly, and had an intense curiosity of world events. As war clouds began to appear over Europe, portending World War II, he followed with interest the speeches of Adolf Hitler and Benito Mussolini. The war that was to engulf the world, call all the Cinabro boys to fight, and bring Maria Brevigileri to him, was many years away, but alert readers could discern the trends in Europe.

So Louis grew into manhood, with the arias of Italian opera sung by Enrico Caruso playing on the radio or phonograph, riding the streetcar to the university while reading in the Chicago papers about the exploits of Al Capone and his gang, and fending for himself and sharing life with his five siblings during the Roaring Twenties. A book was always nearby, and he dabbled in writing plays and articles, dreaming of one day being a playwright. Through all these formative years he lived in the first house the Cinabros ever owned, on Western Avenue in Blue Island.

Louis with his parents—1907

Louis and Antonio in Italy, 1909; girl unidentified

5

The First House

The first house of the Cinabros owned by the family was and is located at 13307 South Western Avenue in Blue Island. This modest dwelling has a history all its own. The subject of a newspaper article in 1979, the house dates from 1840 and is important as the home of the first female born in Blue Island, Eda Ann Jones. On September 1, 1923, Antonio and Rosemary purchased the home from the Nadler family after having rented it since 1921, shortly after their return to America from Muro Lucano. The Cinabro family lived in the house from 1923 through 1940. A small shoemaking store was added as an outbuilding, which no longer stands, although the house with modifications (as of 2003) survives, now known as "The Ramirez House."

According to the newspaper article, "The family enjoyed the spacious front yard, using it for picnics in the summertime." ("The First Girl's Home," *Blue Island Sun Standard,* 1979). The family moved north to 2636 Cochran Street in 1940, a much larger home, but continued to own the Western Avenue house until 1953, in the meantime renting the house to various families until it was purchased by the Ramirez family.

Antoinette remembered how hot the house was in the summertime, particularly on the small second floor, and it must have been cramped indeed with six children and two adults. In two tiny bedrooms upstairs, the five boys shared one room with two beds, three boys sleeping in one bed, and two in the other. Antoinette had the other little room. Downstairs Antonio and Rosemary slept in one bedroom. There was no furnace at first, and heat in the cold Chicago winters was supplied by a stove downstairs.

Antonio (Tony) would go next door to do his trade as shoemaker, and even after the family moved north to Cochran Street, he would walk back to Western Avenue to his work at the shoestore. The young boys would often crawl out of the upstairs windows and jump off the low back roof, and sometimes they would secretly throw clothing through the windows so their parents would not know what they had purchased.

In this small, cramped and modest home, the Cinabro children came of age, went to school, and did odd jobs such as caddying at golf courses, shoeshining, and newspaper delivery. Food was always on the table, and after Rosemary would prepare her specialty dishes the family would eat in the yard on hot summer nights. In this small house the family would greet the arrival of Filomena in 1923, and would witness the start of, and survive, the Great Depression of 1929.

The children of course developed distinctive and independent personalities. Maurice would for a time train as a boxer at Kid Gavelin's Gym, but he never actually fought in the boxing ring. He would nevertheless develop a strong, stocky and muscular physique, combined with a unique and biting sense of humor. Sometime during the family's stay at the house on Western Avenue Maurice would suffer head injuries in an accident when a car or truck struck him as he was walking on the street. Louis would recall that the injuries were serious but not life-threatening.

Antoinette was very disciplined and hard-working, shared her brother Louis' academic interests and love of languages, and did very well in high school. She was a strong, hard-working and helpful assistant to her mother. Of the children, Armand was perhaps the most socially gregarious, outgoing, and adventuresome. He was dashing, masculine and popular with the girls.

Henry, born in 1922 and fifteen years younger than Louis, was always considered the "baby" by his older siblings. A good-looking boy, he was very sociable and friendly, and developed a charming and sunny personality. He was adored by his mother, and looked after by all the siblings. Louis would call him "Sweet Hank."

Animals were loved by the Cinabros and the family cats "Tommy" and "Mike" shared in all the activities. The cats loved the Western Avenue house and would wander back even after the family moved to Cochran Street.

The house where the children came of age, today sits on a quiet dead end street situated in a historic district called "Olde Western Avenue," the original Western Avenue having been diverted on to a causeway. In the 1920s and 1930s the house, however, fronted Western Avenue, a very important and busy thoroughfare, affording traffic, both pedestrian and vehicular, for Tony's shoe business. One can still picture where the little shoestore stood, in the front corner of the yard facing the street. Now it is a quiet yard covered with grass. Next door is an old tavern and restaurant which once belonged to a dear family friend named Helen Sadunas, who ran the business with her brother Albert, after inheriting it from her family.

6

Filomena

Filomena was a family name of Rosemary Pacella's family. She had at least one aunt by that name who lived in Albany, New York, apparently having come to America as part of the same wave of immigration that brought Antonio, although the time and details of this aunt's arrival and her family circumstances are unknown.

When the last child, a baby girl, arrived in the Cinabro family, in the fall of 1923, Rosemary must have been proud to name her second daughter Filomena. Antoinette, being the only girl with five brothers, was overjoyed. She recalled how happy she was to have a baby sister, and she told her parents how she was looking forward to walking the little girl in a baby carriage. She remembered looking at the infant in her cradle and seeing her eyes blink.

But Antoinette's hopes and wishes were not to be. The baby developed pneumonia, or had a congenital disease. Within three months, she died. Antoinette remembered seeing her mother kiss the child in her coffin. Tony paid $72.00 on December 18, 1923, to properly bury the child, and also paid $10.00 for a flower arrangement. The child was buried in Mt. Olivet Cemetery in Mt. Greenwood on 111th Street, not far from Blue Island, on what must have been a cold, snowy day, with all the family present. The death of this child especially affected Antoinette deeply. It took Tony until April of the following year to pay off the burial expenses. But the family never placed a marker on little Filomena's grave. With the arrival of the Great Depression in 1929, and other needs of the large family, it did not happen. It did not represent a lack of love, so much as a need to meet other more pressing economic realities.

In 2003, almost eighty years after her death, Filomena's grave, after much searching, was rediscovered and a proper marker was placed in memory of this almost forgotten but loved child, who lies in a cemetery removed from where her parents rest. If family members visit Holy Sepulchre Cemetery to honor the graves of where most of the Cinabros lie, they can visit Filomena in Mt. Olivet Cemetery down the road a few miles. She lies near several other children also of that era who died in infancy or at a young age, but they remain in unmarked graves.

7

Louis—The Early Years

Louis had to leave the academic world to enter the job market at the height of the Great Depression. He first worked after graduation from the University of Chicago as a language translator for perhaps one or two years (probably part time) for some private agencies, including the William McSurely Agency in Chicago. He would translate scientific and literary articles from foreign language publications and magazines. He soon left this work to join the Illinois State Emergency Relief Commission, where he became a caseworker, taking care of a caseload of families receiving state relief (welfare). He would interview the families, and administer the relief according to data collected from field work. He found this work interesting but the pay was very low. Then the calling that really was his life's passion found him taking a teaching job in Puerto Rico, in 1936, probably in San Juan. He taught in high school in Puerto Rico, teaching English, science and French. There is very little else that is known or documented about this period. This was his first extended experience away from his family and home.

What can be said with certainty is that eventually he met and became engaged to a Puerto Rican woman. Nothing is known about who she was, or what happened to the relationship. It was a serious commitment for him, because a ring was purchased during what must have been stringent economic circumstances. He even went so far as to buy furniture, I was told, but virtually everything that happened is lost in time as to why or when this ended. His fluency in Spanish undoubtedly helped him meet the local girls. He had become a young man of great charm and wit, with a shock of black hair, piercing dark eyes, a sharp intellect, a mastery of several languages, and a keen appreciation of female beauty. He loved conversation and had an engaging personality. Though he could fall into moods of sadness, he was most often very sociable and interested in the events and world around him.

By this time teaching had become very much a vocation that Louis felt most comfortable in, but the economics of a teaching career in that era, when teachers were not paid a living wage, the advent of World War II, and other forces would combine to keep him from ever making this a full time, permanent career.

It is unknown exactly why or when he left Puerto Rico after teaching two years to return to the United States. The end of his relationship with his fiance in Puerto Rico may have had something to do with his decision to return, but economics must have also had much to do with it. Additionally, Blue Island, and his family, were never far from his thoughts. He must have written home a great deal, and thought often of his family. He would all his life write letters and postcards to friends, but his family was first in his heart.

8

The Great Depression

On Thursday, October 24, 1929, the New York Stock Exchange lost four billion dollars in value. By 1932 the banking system had collapsed. Eventually, unemployment in the United States would reach 25 percent. But statistics alone do not tell the story. America had entered a period in which the national psyche was shaken. Louis would recount that bankers would commit suicide by throwing themselves out of windows. Men would survive by selling apples on street corners.

Louis was still in college when the trauma of this event unfolded, ending the carefree and happy "Roaring Twenties." It is impossible today to realize what happened to America, and to families like the Cinabros. There was no federal insurance protection for bank savings accounts. When the economy shattered, many banks just closed their doors. The entire family savings of Tony and Rosemary, about $700.00, was lost completely at a bank that failed, and the money they so painstakingly earned was never recovered. The blow was enormous.

In the small white house on Western Avenue, the crowded family made ends meet with the boys doing odd jobs and Tony continuing with his modest shoe-repair business. Food was always on the table, but there were no luxuries, no vacations, no cars, and little for "fun" or entertainment. The one thing that is not in dispute is that the Cinabro family never took a penny of welfare, or "relief" as it was called in those days. Tony was a proud man, and the work ethic that was instilled in all the children was revealed every day.

Rosemary, as ruler of the hearth and kitchen, summoned all her skills as a cook to keep the family of growing children fed. Antoinette remembered eating meals consisting of dandelions picked in the yard and cooked in a salad, with boiled potatoes, eggs in tomato sauce, and frequent macaroni. The loss of their life savings did not stop Tony and Rosemary from raising the family, maintaining the house, and making sure that everyone stayed out of trouble. Not one of the children was ever in trouble with the law, though excuses could have been made given the severe economic hardships. The boys went to school and brought home whatever money they could earn from selling newspapers or shining shoes.

Louis would talk of the "Depression Years" frequently and until his old age. Jobs were next to impossible to find. Until Franklin Roosevelt and the "New Deal," the country was in a state of psychological as well as financial malaise. Louis would remind everyone that this was an event that could someday repeat itself. In reality, the pain of those troubled years would never leave him, nor most members of his generation.

Maurice, like all the siblings, struggled hard to find jobs during those years. He recalled one job he had, in a factory or warehouse, that lasted just a few weeks. When he was let go, all he was given was one ham to take home for dinner. There was no unemployment benefit, no severance package, and no thanks. He would remember some people thought he was lucky to get a ham.

As a schoolgirl, Antoinette only had one simple dress to wear to school every day. When she asked Rosemary for a second dress she was sternly told there was no money. Antoinette would endure the looks from other students and swallow her pride. It did not deter her from being a good student and developing a strong personality.

The depression years changed Louis's thinking and personality in many subtle ways. He would always believe in saving money and he was always most frugal, almost spartan, in his personal habits. He never splurged or spent money extravagantly. He would turn off every electric light that was not being used, and would be careful not to leave any lights turned on when the house was empty. He appreciated the value of money, and of how difficult it could be to earn enough to survive. Thus, when after he returned from Puerto Rico a teaching opportunity presented itself at an elite military academy in Indiana, he was grateful to "jump at the chance" as he used to say. The Culver years would represent an end to the immediate economic challenges for Louis, just as the country itself was pulling out of the Depression.

9

Louis—Culver Years

The first superintendent of the Culver Military Academy in Culver, Indiana, was Alexander ("Fred") Fleet, a Virginian, an officer and veteran of Robert E. Lee's famed Army of Northern Virginia. He accompanied General Lee to Appomattox, and after the Civil War he graduated from the University of Virginia and then began a teaching career. Very much a scholar and citizen soldier, as Louis would aspire to become, Lt. Fleet eventually organized a military academy in Missouri, and then he subsequently went to Culver, where from 1896 he would preside until 1910. It was to this prestigious, elite school, in north-central Indiana, about a three hour auto ride from Blue Island, that Louis came in September of 1939, to begin teaching French and Spanish. This was his next calling after teaching in the high schools of Puerto Rico. It must have been especially rewarding for him to obtain this position, and the local Blue Island newspaper took note. The contract he signed called for a salary of $1,720.00 for the academic year, of which $320.00 would be charged for room and board to be furnished by the academy.

Culver is located in a picturesque college-like campus on the shores of Lake Maxinkuchee, due south of South Bend, Indiana. It is now known as the Culver Academies and is coeducational, but in 1939 it was a private boys only prep school known as the Culver Military Academy. It had equestrian, boating, and other superb athletic facilities, and a demanding academic curriculum. It was stepped in tradition, and the campus had a number of memorials to its sons who had fallen in America's wars.

That Culver was and is a special place is reflected in the fact that two Hollywood movies have been made about it. The first film was called *Tom Brown of Culver* and was made in 1932. Tyrone Power made his screen debut in this story, about a boy receiving a scholarship to the famed academy during the Depression years. In 1939, the year Louis began his career at the academy, the movie *the Spirit of Culver* was filmed, starring such famous actors as Jackie Cooper and Tim Holt.

At first an adjustment was necessary given that Louis had no military background and came from a comparatively economically disadvantaged immigrant family. He was not a stern disciplinarian. But it soon became apparent that Culver would form a significant chapter in Louis' life. He formed friendships which would last a lifetime, and lived in the barrack with many of the cadets. He demonstrated loyalty and a cooperative spirit, and as Major Leland stated, "This man 'grows on me.' " Culver influenced and developed Louis, as he would influence his cadets. Louis's duties included inspection and supervision duties as well as teaching, and he helped supervise the campus newspaper writing.

An important person with whom he came in contact was Colonel J. S. Fleet, the son of Alexander Fleet. They engaged in correspondence which lasted during the war years, and in one letter written to Colonel Fleet in 1942, Louis expressed the following: "I am deeply appreciative of my wonderful experience acquired while working at Culver. It was of untold value to me, because Culver not only 'makes' boys, it also has an incalculable and beneficial influence upon instructors there. I hope to be able to offer my services to Culver in the future. At any rate, I will always be ready to serve it." He would remain at Culver teaching three full years, and also in the summer of 1942.

The pictures show him at ease with and very fond of his cadets, and he readily partook of the social functions including a huge dinner dance held on Thanksgiving, which featured 3,000 people attending, and which generated a newspaper article telling of brother Armand's attendance. Culver attracted the elite of the nation, and Louis would remember meeting the famous Hollywood actress Carole Lombard, who married Clark Gable. He seemed very happy in the Culver environment, and were it not for the advent of World War II, it is quite likely he would have remained indefinitely, doing what he liked best, teaching foreign languages to a high-caliber of students in a military environment with strict discipline. He formed a friendship with a newly arrived art professor at Culver, Warner Williams, who became a talented sculptor, and the two corresponded regularly for the rest of their lives.

That September of 1939 was pivotal in world history. Adolf Hitler invaded Poland on the very day Louis began at Culver, September 1, and the war cloud which had been gathering over Europe erupted into a world war. Although America would not enter the war until Pearl Harbor, many of the cadets he taught undoubtedly would go off to war. One poignant picture shows Louis posing with several cadets near a cannon on the Culver campus in front of Legion Memorial Hall one snowy winter day, symbolizing more than anyone could know the portentous events that were coming.

31

The effects of the Great Depression were beginning to dissipate in the mid-1930s under the policies of President Franklin D. Roosevelt. For the Cinabro family this meant that though the family would never know affluence, some of the economic hardships they faced would lessen. In 1940 while Louis was at Culver they would move the family home from the little house on Western Avenue in Blue Island to a more spacious brick home north of the old home at 2636 Cochran Street in Blue Island. The brick home had four bedrooms and a full two stories and must have seemed much more accommodating to the still large family living under one roof. Antoinette remembered how happy Tony was in the new house, and how he would walk the street talking to all the neighbors. The family was able to keep the old white house and rented it to others until 1953 when it was finally sold. This reflected the hard work and thrifty ways of the family, enabling them to gradually but steadily move away from poverty and "hard times," despite losing all the money they had saved during the Depression.

It seems Tony was a very gregarious and sociable person, and, like his father, Louis acquired and kept these characteristics in his adulthood. He loved to meet and talk with people, and followed current events with a keen intellectual curiosity. He loved to write letters, especially to his family and to his mother, and continued his avid reading of great literature. It cannot be overstated how books were the passion of his life, along with music. He developed a strong physical constitution, and though short of stature he was capable of great endurance, being an early riser like his mother, and working long hours. He would always love to walk, and walking three to five miles a day was nothing to him. He never drove an automobile. He made a trip to New York City, in the summer of 1939, probably to visit relatives of Rosemary, and he looked quite fashionably dressed and even dashing in the photos.

Though he never liked the cold weather, he would endure the hard, icy and damp winters of Chicago and Northern Indiana. Tony too endured these hard winters. Tony continued working daily in his little shoe repair business, and always kept detailed records of his accounts. The account entries stopped suddenly in March of 1941. He had gone for a walk, then developed a cold, which later led to pneumonia. Though Henry felt that perhaps his father had breathed too much dust in all the years of making and repairing shoes, he had an asthmatic condition which left his lungs vulnerable. Tony died after a brief hospitalization at the age of sixty-one, never having "retired" and working almost till the day he died. One cold day in March of 1941 Louis requested a leave of absence from Culver and made the trip to Blue Island, to be at his father's funeral mass at St. Benedict Church in Blue Island, and then to the burial at Holy Sepulchre Cemetery, a different cemetery than where infant daughter Filomena was buried. Tony, Antonio, this man who had come so far from his native land, who fought in World War I, who had proudly become an American citizen, who had raised six children, who had suffered through the Great Depression, had endured intimidation by the "Black Hand," and who never had a real "vacation" in the modern sense, died quietly and peacefully. He was buried in his adopted country with the quiet and unpretentious dignity which symbolized his life. After the funeral Louis returned to Culver, and despite the advent of the war, he never forgot Culver and he would continue to correspond with Colonel Gregory, the Superintendent, and with Colonel Fleet.

33

Louis in New York City, summer, 1939

In front of Legion Hall with his cadets, 1940

10

Louis—The War Years

On December 7, 1941, a Sunday afternoon, a few months after Tony died, Antoinette was washing walls at 2636 Cochran Street with Rosemary when a news bulletin on the radio announced that the Japanese had attacked Pearl Harbor. They turned to each other and said, "It is war." And so America became engulfed in the massive conflict that had already affected all of Europe and much of Asia. For Louis, World War II would be in many ways the defining period of his life. He would travel the world and meet his bride. He loved Army life. In a 1943 wartime letter to his mentor Colonel Fleet at Culver he would write: "Army life is certainly dynamic, Col. Fleet, and I like it." He would begin an odyssey in May of 1943 that would take him to Scotland, England, French Morocco, Algeria, Tunisia, Sicily and Italy.

All five Cinabro brothers would be called to serve their country in the war. Maurice, Henry and Louis would fight in the European theatre, Armand would fight in the South Pacific, and Art would serve in the United States. Though Tony had not lived to see all this, Rosemary would place five stars in the window at the Cochran Street family home. Antoinette remembered how upset Rosemary was when Henry, the youngest son, was called, and was the last to leave. It is not an exaggeration to say that Cinabro family gave as much as anyone to the war. It is an undeniable record of pride, patriotism in the true sense, and honor. Among them, the boys would earn a Purple Heart, three Silver Battle Stars, and one Bronze Battle Star. Theirs were not "cushy" rear echelon duties. Maurice and Henry would serve with George Patton's Third Army, fighting across France. Henry would fight at the "Battle of the Bulge." Armand would see heavy combat in the Pacific. The story of Louis would be that of General Mark Clark's Fifth Army.

Louis was inducted on November 21 of 1942 at Fort Sheridan, Illinois, after having taught summer school that year at Culver. As a private he first entered a training battalion and did his basic training at Miami Beach, Florida. He then went to Greeley, Colorado, where he entered the Army Air Forces Clerical School at Fort Logan. His knowledge of languages brought him to the attention of the military command, which felt that his services to the country could best be utilized in military intelligence. In February, 1943, he went to Camp Ritchie, Maryland, to the Military Intelligence School, and eventually to the Order of Battle School at the Pentagon in Washington, D.C. He entered active duty on May 17, 1943, as a censorship officer, and was commissioned as a second lieutenant in the Army. While at Camp Ritchie he travelled to Gettysburg, Pennsylvania, and wrote a postcard to Rosemary describing the "sacred city of Gettysburg" where that momentous Civil War battle was fought. No matter where he was during the war, letters and cards home to Rosemary were very important.

In a newspaper article which appeared in his hometown Blue Island paper, the *Sun Standard,* in 1943, he described his training and duties, which included photography, interrogation of prisoners of war, and night problems of reconnaissance in the mountains of Pennsylvania and Maryland. He found army life and work "fascinating" and there is no evidence of griping or discontent. He hoped to be assigned to an army air corps unit (the air force was still not a separate branch in those days).

On May 29, 1943, he was ordered to the North African theater as a military intelligence officer. In November of 1942 the United States had begun the invasion of North Africa, in what was up to that time the biggest amphibious operation of the war. General Eisenhower had led an Anglo-American army to the shores of French North Africa. Though Rommel's Afrika Corps of the German Army had been fighting British forces through 1942, America entered the North African campaign late that year. This would be the first of the campaigns that Louis would be in.

By April of 1943 the British Eighth Army under Montgomery had captured Tripoli and reached Tunisia. On May 7, 1943, American forces took Bizerte, and the British took the city of Tunis. Shortly after this, Louis arrived, after first flying to Scotland in a C-54 transport plane. The route he flew happened to be the same one in which the famed actor Leslie Howard of *Gone with the Wind* had been shot down two days earlier by German planes. Lieutenant Cinabro left Scotland after a few days and landed in French Morocco, and he began interrogating German and Italian prisoners of war. He worked closely with British intelligence officers, and remembered that the German prisoners, especially the S.S. officers, would reveal very little information.

The Fifth Army would be his home and his pride during the war. The Fifth Army was activated at Oujda, French Morocco, on January 5, 1943, under the command of Lieutenant General Mark Clark. Its shoulder patch and emblem showed the outline of a mosque, symbolic of its origins in North Africa. It was the first U.S. Army to initiate combat on the European mainland, on September 9, 1943, at Salerno, and made a name for itself at the battles of Anzio, Monte Cassino, and the Rapido River.

The sands, customs, and exotic culture of North Africa would leave impressions on him that would last a lifetime. He always took opportunities to visit local museums and bazaars, and wrote a long letter to his hometown newspaper which was published as an article. This flowing account illustrates the zest for life and the intellectual curiosity which he always displayed, no matter what the circumstances. As he stated, "I see no reason whatsoever for griping of any kind." He loved what he was doing, at a time when historical events were unfolding. Though he thought of his beloved home in Blue Island often, and even memorized the family letters he would receive, he could state honestly and without braggadocio, "I am right in the midst of momentous happenings, and now I realize how thrillingly fascinating life can be, and what must the moth feel when it is drawn inexorably towards the flame."

The *Blue Island Sun-Standard* went out of its way to publish this lengthy letter on October 28, 1943, with the editor noting how "even some of the boys in service will appreciate it as well as the folks here at home." Lt. Cinabro described his long and perilous journey to Scotland, and then the twelve-hour flight to French Morocco. In the letter, he examined and vividly described the local customs and culture, waxing eloquently and exhibiting a fascination with all he had encountered. He came into contact with a richly colorful and diverse number of people. To quote further from this letter: "Charming French girls, prisoners of war, little Arabs in the remote Arab villages of Algeria and Tunisia, British, Free French, Senegalese and Foreign Legion soldiers, all, all inquire about Ginger Rogers, Popeye, and Donald Duck when you stop and talk to them. The last time I visited El Kairouan, an Arab Sacred City, I spent half an hour telling little Arabs who scarcely understood some french all about Boris Karloff and Pluto. The role of the movies in winning friendship and admiration for the U.S.A. here is incalculable."

He would recall meeting in North Africa Creighton Abrams, who much later would be the commander of all U.S. forces in Vietnam in the late 1960s. He would meet and form friendships in the army that lasted until his dying days. He never would forget the army, and his travels, and the adventure of it all. He would see French Morocco, Algeria, and Tunisia. He would make short trips out of Africa to select prisoners of war to be interrogated, and eventually became a supply officer with an interrogation of Prisoners of War Company at headquarters in Algiers. He coordinated, re-wrote and disseminated reports from the combat zones.

The American and British allies on July 10, 1943, launched the invasion of the island of Sicily, and soon the island was taken from the Italian and German forces. On September 3, 1943, Italy surrendered, but the main part of the country was soon taken over by the German army and in effect became a seized and occupied part of Hitler's Third Reich. In the first Allied invasion of mainland Europe, on September 9, 1943, General Clark's Fifth Army, along with British and Canadian forces, landed at Salerno, south of Naples, and thus began the long drive up the boot of Italy to Rome. Lieutenant Cinabro was in the second wave at Salerno, and continued his duties as an intelligence officer. He served for a time in Sicily, but most of his assignments would be on the mainland of Italy, near the birthplace of Tony and Rosemary, and near where he spent some years of his childhood. There is no record that he visited Muro Lucano during his World War Ii service in Italy, but one can imagine his thoughts as he arrived in the uniform of an American officer to help liberate an occupied land.

He would write long and frequent letters to his family, especially to Rosemary, all throughout the war. He would send many postcards, often from the places he had visited in North Africa and Italy. Family, and Blue Island, were never far from his thoughts, and his concern and care for his brothers is also evident in his writings.

What became known as the Rome–Arno campaign would be the most significant phase of the war for him. He would be part of the Fifth Army in its progression towards Rome, with the goal of liberating that occupied capital of Italy. He would sustain jaw and head injuries in a jeep accident during the campaign, when a jeep he was riding rolled over during the march on Rome, which necessitated significant dental work. He would forever remember the sound of the famous German "88" gun, used as an anti-aircraft and anti-tank weapon, one of the most versatile weapons of the war. He eventually switched from prisoner interrogation to censorship.

His service record shows that he earned the European Theater Ribbon with a Bronze Battle Star, and six service bars with the victory medal. He also received a formal written commendation after the war. His work in intelligence brought him close to the front lines, and he was under enemy fire. The allies kept pushing forward north to Rome, and on June 4, 1944, the Fifth Army liberated Rome. By August of 1944, he would earn promotion to First Lieutenant. The battle for Rome, and the life changing events which occurred, form the next part of this story, when he would meet Maria Breviglieri, of Mantua, Italy.

Louis in 1943

Fifth Army shoulder patch

11

Maria Breviglieri

The town in Northern Italy from whence Maria came is as far from Muro Lucano by distance geographically as it is culturally. This ancient city in the Po River Valley of Lombardy province is mentioned in Shakespeare's *Romeo and Juliet* as the refuge to which Romeo fled from Verona, and it is also the setting for Verdi's opera, *Rigoletto.* It is bordered on three sides by lakes formed from the Mincio River. It began as an Etruscan settlement, founded by that ancient and mysterious civilization which always fascinated Maria. Later it became a Roman town, and was the birthplace of the great Latin poet Virgil, who flourished under the reign of the Roman emperor Augustus.

Mantua (Mantova in Italian) had an even more glittering history as the seat of a great and influential Italian Renaissance family, the Gonzagas, who flourished from 1328 to 1708. They built great palaces in the town, which was a city-state in those days, and the palaces, full of art and paintings, can be seen today. Maria was always conscious and proud of her Lombard and Mantovan heritage, and she loved to read and speak of her hometown always.

In this place she was born on March 13, 1922, the daughter of Romeo Breviglieri and his wife Ermetina, nee Consoli. Romeo was a skilled craftsman and carpenter, and Ermetina received a university degree from the University of Modena, which in those times in Italy was a significant achievement for a woman. For Maria, life was immediately going to challenge her. Ermetina died just a few days after giving birth to Maria, leaving Romeo to care for the infant Maria as well as her older brother Nando. Romeo could not care for these small children, and Nando was sent to be raised by relatives near Milan, and Maria was given to her paternal aunt Virginia (known as Aunt Ginia) who would raise Maria. The death of her mother would always affect Maria, and she would speak of never having a mother to care for her and to love her. Aunt Ginia gave her loving care, and did all she could, but Maria always felt in some ways as an orphan. Romeo would remarry and have two more children, Stelio and Teresa. Both Stelio and Teresa would be considered by Maria as her full brother and sister despite their having different mothers.

Though Romeo did not raise Maria, she would always love her father. She never held it against him, and understood his limitations. She would seek his advice when necessary, and he would give what he could when he could. Maria had to rapidly develop a philosophy of life to survive what for many would have been undeniably difficult circumstances. Though she never knew affluence, (she only had one doll as a child), she never felt sorry for herself, she always was able to find happiness in the smallest things, fended for herself with very little, and had an unbounded joy of living. Though life would not always be fair to her, Maria was given a unique gift that helped her survive, and that was the ability to find happiness with little or no material possessions. If it was a butterfly flying in the air, a firefly lighting the night, or reading a romantic novel, Maria could find happiness. She did not know the meaning of the word "bitter."

She attended the local schools in Mantua, but she could not advance to the university level because of lack of funds in the family. She clearly would have had the capacity to attend college, and if she had lived in America in a different era she would have excelled. She had a quick wit, a vivacious personality, and loved to read, like the man she would marry. She was never a braggart, and was very humble, but at the same time proud and independent. The one thing she could afford with a few lire to do while growing up was watching American movies dubbed in Italian, and she loved Shirley Temple. One of her favorite movies was *The Scartlet Pimpernel,* made in 1934 and starring Leslie Howard, the same actor who starred in *Gone with the Wind* and who died in 1943 just two days before Louis flew to Scotland on the same flight path. America was a distant land of the movies, and Maria never really dreamed, or desired, to go to America.

She was slight of stature, but she was active and physical growing up from childhood. She developed a certain degree of independence which was compounded by the war, and her experiences in Rome. She was born into a Fascist society, and she wore the uniform when attending the elementary schools in Mantua. Like all idealistic schoolgirls of her age, she was indoctrinated and mesmerized for a time by the charisma of Italian dictator Benito Mussolini, who for a time thundered unto the world stage even before Adolf Hitler.

Aunt Ginia was loving but strict, and Maria knew manual labor even as a child, washing dishes at age nine and caring for an ailing grandmother. She would read books by candlelight, and would love to do gymnastic exercises, recalling she was really a "tomboy" as a child. She would watch Tarzan movies and swing from trees calling out his yell.

By the time she had completed what was the equivalent of high school, she knew she could not afford to go further with her formal education. Much like Antonio Cinabro, her schooling would come not in the classroom but in the struggle for survival in the work world. This she confronted at the age of eighteen, when the family decided it would be best if Maria left Mantua to move to Rome, to find a job and make her way. This was a defining moment for her. Except for a couple of brief trips home during and after the war, she would go first to Rome, and then to Venice, then to America, before she ever returned to Mantua for an extended period. She left Mantua by train for the ride south to Rome, with many tears and much anxiety. The year was 1939, about the same time that Louis left Blue Island to start his teaching career at Culver.

She had very little with her, one suitcase, a few lire, and no job. She was going to live with a cousin and her family in Rome, and this was all. She was very homesick at first, and very lonely. But soon, her instinct for survival, her basic resiliency, and her philosophy of life enabled her to acclimate to the new life she found.

Rome was as far removed from Mantua as if it were a foreign city in a different nation. This ancient, axis capital, so full of history, churches, ruins and beauty, and so much at the center of the world stage in the late 1930s, only second to Berlin in the eyes of the world, would change Maria forever, and in ways she could never imagine.

She soon found work as a stenographer in a munitions company in Rome. This would be her job throughout the war. She befriended several people who would protect her and watch over her, the most important being Miss Mazzei, an older Roman lady who worked at the same company, and who became, in many respects, almost as an aunt or mother to Maria. Maria always used to say that she found kind people to help her, and Miss Mazzei was certainly one of those special persons. Their memories together during the war years would always remain in Maria's soul, and she would recall Miss Mazzei with affection to her dying days.

When she arrived in 1939 Rome was still under the Fascist government of Benito Mussolini. Maria would recall going to the Palazzo Venezia to see the Italian dictator stand on his balcony and speak to his nation. She saw Mussolini many times, and was part of many large crowds listening to his speeches. When the war began with Hitler's invasion of Poland in 1939, on the same day Louis started teaching at Culver, Maria was in Rome, still very much a part of the majority of Italian society still trusting in their government. Though her father Romeo was anti-fascist, when Maria arrived in Rome she still believed in Mussolini. She did not dislike him, and did not think of him as evil or bad for Italy. This would all change very soon.

She would ride the streetcar to work at the munitions company, and her honest and vivacious personality soon made her less lonely and more confident. She became more worldly and more cosmopolitan living in such a large and diverse city. She came into contact with a different culture than Mantua, and soon loved Rome and her life there, even thought it was not pretentious or ostentatious.

Through 1941 and into 1942 Rome had still not felt the effects of the war in earnest, though food rationing began soon. Hunger would always be with her through the war years. Meat became more of a rarity, and she was never very well nourished. This would worsen after the German occupation.

1943 brought dramatic changes to the fortunes of the Fascist government of Mussolini and to the people of Rome. The first of the life threatening experiences she would encounter happened to Maria on July 19, 1943, when the first air raid to hit Rome occurred. Allied bombers, B–17s and B–24s, struck the railroad marshalling yards at San Lorenzo. Maria lived with her relatives in an apartment building nearby. She was at work when the air raid happened. When she went home from work, all her residential area was destroyed. There was nothing but rubble and body parts, and Maria would repeatedly recall seeing the arms and legs protruding from the rubble. Her relatives had escaped injury, but her shelter with them was gone. She somehow found a new home, with Miss Mazzei and others helping her. She would never forget this air raid, though there would be others. She began to walk several kilometers to work once the streetcar lines had been destroyed.

In September of 1943, Mussolini was deposed. The king of Italy then surrendered the country and tried to remove Italy from the war. Very soon thereafter the Germans decided to occupy the city rather than turn it over to the Americans. Italian partisans and some soldiers fought to keep the Germans from entering the city. Despite some heroic resistance at a place in Rome called Porta San Paolo on September 10, the Germans soon overcame the Italian fighters and thus began the German occupation of the city.

12

Rome, 1944–1945

In the wonderfully detailed and long overdue book called *The Battle for Rome,* written by Robert Katz, published by Simon & Schuster in 2003, the story of the German occupation of Rome is depicted. One should read this book to acquire a sense of what life was like for Maria during those days. Much of the chronology and history of some of the events recounted here are taken from this work.

In the fall of 1943, Field Marshal Albert Kesseiring took over control of the city, and the Romans had to adapt to life in a Nazi-controlled environment. Maria continued her work at the munitions company after the German takeover. She would walk to work, perform her duties, and occasionally treat herself to a movie when she could do so, without violating the curfew. Food was rationed and amenities were scarce. She was never overnourished to begin with, and during her years in Rome, Maria probably developed a degree of malnutrition, given the lack of meat, fruit and other necessities. An active black market formed for scarce food and other needs. The Germans appropriated most of the meat, and many of the cows were shipped to Germany. Maria was always hungry. She recalled one incident that illustrates this. One day after work she was approached by a man who told her to meet him at a certain place if she wanted to get fresh meat, from a cow which was stolen from the Germans. Maria agreed to do this but took a great risk. She did not know what would happen, or what would be asked in return.

As she told the story, she went to the place at the appointed time. True to his word, the man was there and secretly distributed fresh cuts of meat from the slaughtered cow to a few Romans. He asked for nothing in return. He may have been a partisan or just a patriotic Roman trying to help his fellow citizens during the occupation. In any event, Maria was able to take home fresh meat for the first time in a long time. The Germans apparently did not catch the patriot doing this. Maria used to recount that much of the flour distributed during rationing was mixed with concrete which was used to make bread. She never could get enough to eat.

Maria was not an active partisan such as those who are described in *The Battle for Rome* by Robert Katz. However, she worked for a munitions company and during the German occupation this became a center where partisans, including her two bosses, both Italian generals, became active. The extent of her knowledge of these activities is unknown, but as an astute person who had developed "street sense" she certainly knew they were involved. The sensitive nature of the production of munitions by a company in time of war made this the focus of much German interest and curiosity.

Maria became used to seeing the Germans all over Rome, standing on streetcorners holding their machine guns. One day she passed on the street Field Marshall Kesseiring himself, and he acknowledged her as she passed. Maria had become an attractive, petite young woman, with dark eyes and a vivacious and curious personality.

On March 23, 1944, there occurred the incident which forms much of the story of *The Battle for Rome.* In the Via Rasella a huge explosion suddenly rocked the streets when Italian partisans threw a bomb at marching German S.S. Police troops. The 11th Company of the Bozen S.S. 3d Battalion suffered thirty-two fatalities and many injuries. The reaction of Hitler and the German command in Rome was swift and furious. From his headquarters in East Prussia, Hitler ordered that ten Italians for every German who died were to be executed. Among those taken into custody was General Martelli, one of Maria's bosses, and a man whom she admired and respected greatly. It is not known whether General Martelli was involved, or how much he knew. He, along with many other Italians, was rounded up and put in cells in Via Tasso.

When the explosion happened, Maria was watching a movie in a movie theater not far from Via Rasella. She recounted how the lights were suddenly turned on, and everyone was told to leave. She almost went into the street, not knowing what had happened, when an Italian man grabbed her and pushed her back into the theater lobby. She saw many German soldiers in the square rounding up people just after the attack. What would have happened to her had she gone outside always remained in her mind and memory for the rest of her life.

General Martelli and 334 other people were taken from prison cells at Via Tasso and on March 24 brought to caverns called the Ardeatine Caves, where they were brutally shot by German forces. Their bodies were piled and entombed there. Soon word spread of the atrocity, and much later the world would learn of it. Now the caves are a memorial to the slain patriots. Maria was so greatly affected by this, and what happened to her bosses, that she spoke of it repeatedly. This searing experience would never leave her.

But she survived it, and continued her work for the company, which managed to continue its production despite the unbelievable circumstances. There grew a pervading sense among the Italian population that it was just a matter of time before the American and British allies coming toward Rome from the south of Italy would be victorious and liberate Rome. Maria would hear and see German soldiers on the streetcorners of Rome, the average soldiers and not the S.S., spit and say "Hitler kaput," to express their disgust and hope that the war would end.

While all this was happening in Rome, the Americans and allies were moving north, and Lieutenant Cinabro passed through Naples, that sprawling port city from where Antonio had departed Italy in 1903, and which was where Antoinette was later born. Finally, the Gustav line held by the Germans was broken, and the Fifth Army marched on Rome.

Maria remembered vividly the day the Germans abandoned Rome, on June 4, 1944. She saw the long columns of soldiers, carrying all their supplies as well as much material stolen from Italy, winding their way through the streets in a dispirited and dejected way. She recalled the empty looks on the soldiers' faces, and how all was silent, with malnourished onlookers staring at the Germans but betraying no emotion. Fortunately, the city was spared destruction as the German army left without resorting to a "scorched earth" policy.

How different and bright the mood was after twenty-four hours. In came the Americans, and Maria stood in a huge throng cheering the Fifth Army as it entered Rome. It was June 5, 1944. The soldiers would throw candies and chocolates to people who had been used to small amounts of bread and very little meat. She was right next to the long lines of American soldiers as they came down the streets, in their trucks and tanks and jeeps and on foot. She always wore sunglasses when she was young. These sunglasses must have been special, for they attracted the attention of many passing American soldiers, many of whom stopped to ask Maria if they could buy them from her. She refused to part with them. As she was watching the soldiers, an American soldier approached her and grabbed her glasses without saying anything and walked off. Maria was not afraid of an army, allied or otherwise, and made her feelings known as to this unfair theft of her sunglasses. An American officer retrieved her sunglasses, and apologized to her. This tiny incident in the middle of the war was a small example of Maria's spirit and independence.

Lieutenant Cinabro entered Rome shortly after the combat units of the Fifty Army. He was attached to a company headquarters unit, and was working at this stage of the war primarily in censorship, in G–2. When the headquarters unit entered Rome he was a special report writer for the company, and headed a translation section. He would gather civilian mail, newspapers, telegraph, telephone and cable materials, and translate and disseminate this information to higher headquarters. After he left North Africa he was no longer primarily involved in prisoner of war interrogation.

On June 6, 1944, the day after Rome was liberated, the allied invasion of Normandy took place, and the Americans and British allies started a second western front in Europe. Brothers Henry and Maurice Cinabro later followed the landings, and they would join General Patton's Third Army, which would make a name for itself thundering across France toward Germany.

Henry would be in the 87th Division and it would become known as the "Golden Acorn" Division for its shoulder patch. The division arrived in France in November of 1944, and would go across France, Belgium, Luxemburg, and into Germany. Henry served as a medic, but he alone guarded forty German prisoners after one battle. He eventually would earn three Silver Battle Stars. The 87th Division would meet with the Russian army and would free the city of Koblentz.

Maurice would be a grenadier and follow Patton's tanks on foot as the Third Army rolled across France. He served in the 4th Division. He would vividly recall the gruesome sight after one battle of seeing many dead German soldiers scattered in a field in France. He would earn the rank of sergeant and participate in the liberation of Paris. Unlike his brothers, Lt. Louis Cinabro would remain in Rome for the balance of the conflict in Europe, serving at headquarters and using his skills with languages to lead the censorship unit.

During his military service Maurice would meet and become a tentmate of a person who later became famous as a member of the "Rat Pack" in Hollywood and Las Vegas. This was Joey Bishop, who became a comedian and movie actor. Years after the war, Maurice and Antoinette would attend a show in Chicago featuring Joey Bishop, who still remembered his wartime buddy with the words: "Hey, Cinabro!"

Maria was feeling the debilitating effects of the war, the rationing, the bombings, the killings, all the uncertainty. Malnutrition was a constant reality, and there came a certain point where she experienced a crisis of spirit. Always a person of faith, though not a regular churchgoer, one night she prayed to God fervently for hope and change. And soon her prayers were answered when she met Lieutenant Cinabro, and a new world opened to her.

Was it love at first sight? For Louis, definitely yes. He would tell his army comrades that once he saw her, if she accepted his invitation to dinner he would marry her. They first saw each other on a Rome street, when a jeep in which he was riding passed her as she was walking home from work. He told his driver to stop and then asked if they could help take her to her destination. Always a person of caution, especially when it came to foreign soldiers, Americans or otherwise, she refused. She did however accept his dinner invitation for a later date. For Maria, love would develop over time.

Their courtship would evolve over a number of months. They would often have dinner at the army commissary, or "PX," then stroll the streets of the vast, ancient city, visiting the ruins of ancient Rome, and of the Etruscans, that lost civilization that so fascinated Maria. Louis's mastery of the Italian language, which he spoke like a native, won her heart, along with his scholarly knowledge and intellect. She fell in love, and she learned to sing American songs and learned a few words of English. She continued to work at the munitions company during their courtship, and they would speak of America and the movies, of the war, literature, and the arts. Their activities did not go unnoticed by a group of armed Italian partisans, who one night stopped them in the street and blocked their passage as Louis was walking her home.

Factions of Italian partisans did not favor Italian girls dating American soldiers. This group, and others, had abducted girls and later abused them, doing such things as cutting all their hair as a stigma of shame. They interrogated Louis and Maria for quite some time and would not let them go. For Maria and Louis, this incident could have led to serious consequences. Though he carried a .45 caliber pistol, he did not attempt to fight with this armed group. He used his skill with the Italian language to persuade them that he and Maria were genuinely dating, and that she was with him voluntarily. After much discussion, Maria and Louis were allowed to leave without physical harm. Even with the Nazis gone, Rome could be perilous in 1944. These partisans told Maria she was lucky that Louis spoke Italian as well as he did.

Louis would meet Miss Mazzei, Maria's close friend who still protected her, as well as her co-workers at the company, and Maria in turn was introduced to many of the officers, British and Australian as well as American, who worked with Louis in the intelligence unit. Louis and Maria would visit many places, including the hills and villas in and outside of Rome, to spend an afternoon reading or picnicking. Louis continued his vigorous correspondence with family and friends, and wrote postcards and letters to his mother almost daily. He worried about his brothers, especially young "sweet Hank," and he learned that Armand was in Manila. Armand would earn a Purple Heart and experience the heaviest combat of all the brothers, serving in the Pacific Theater for the war.

The war in Europe finally came to an end in May of 1945, after the Russian siege and conquest of Berlin. Shortly thereafter, on June 9, 1945, Louis and Maria would marry, the Catholic ceremony taking place at Holy Cross of Jerusalem Church in Rome. Maria's co-workers from the company were present, as were many of the army intelligence officers of the Fifth Army. The photos show a very happy couple, with Louis in his uniform and Maria in a simple white dress. For her, life would be transformed beyond her comprehension. Maria, who never had a permanent home, would in a few years find one in America.

Louis soon left the censorship company to join the

University Training Command in Florence, Italy, where he would teach languages, primarily Italian and Spanish, throughout the summer and fall of 1945. They spent time in Florence, and Louis would rejoice in letters and cards home at the opportunity to visit all the art museums and church edifices of that Renaissance city. In Florence they met Claude Bove, an American officer from New York City, and a lifetime friendship would ensue. Claude, like Louis, had an academic and teaching background, and they found much in common. They loved literature and the arts, and would read books and search the city for its special art treasures. Louis eventually rejoined the censorship unit and became acting command officer of the American section of the censorship company, G–2, Allied Force Headquarters, and was ordered to Venice, Italy, where he and Maria would spend an idyllic year.

Maria, Rome, 1943

Louis and Maria in the Rome Hills, circa 1944

13

Venice—1946

From Florence, that Renaissance city full of art and culture, Maria and Louis would travel to Venice, sometime in late 1945 or early 1946. The time they spent together in Venice would always be described by her as the happiest period of her life. The journey there did not start propitiously, as Maria would suffer the air sickness and cold of riding in an army cargo plane, with very little comfort or amenities. But once they arrived, they would be billeted at the Palazzo Venier Dei Leoni, a palace built in the 1750s but never completed. The Allies had appropriated the Palazzo, and there were one or two floors in a beautiful location fronting the Grand Canal of Venice. Along with British and Australian intelligence officers Louis would command the unit that was part of the Allied Force Headquarters in post-war Italy. The country was starting to recover from the effects of the war, and until the nation could "get on its feet" the Allied military presence was necessary and desirable.

Maria would recall for the rest of her days the mellow, relaxing afternoons spent at the Palazzo, a comfortable and serene setting, where there were servants to take care of the officers and their spouses, and where for the first time in her life she knew something of pleasure, and not having to worry whether there was enough food to eat. They would befriend many people with whom they would correspond for the rest of their lives. There was Major Champion from England, Captain Taylor from Australia, and Captain Rich and his wife. Mrs. Rich, Maria and Louis are shown in photos enjoying walks through Venice, and relaxing near the Palazzo and the Grand Canal. It seemed almost a dreamlike interlude from the sometimes harsh reality of what they had both been through in their lives up to that point.

At some time during their stay in Venice, or possibly when they were still in Florence, Maria introduced Louis to her brother Nando, and his wife Iris, in Mantua. It is believed, though this is not certain, that Louis may have also met Maria's father, Romeo. There are no photos or records of this visit.

Nando served in the Italian army during World War II. He was a medical officer and after the war became a pharmacist in Mantua. He was always fiercely patriotic, loved his native land and the city of his birth, and knew much about the history and pageantry of that city of the Gonzagas. He loved politics and world events, was curious like his sister about all things, and was close to Maria, whom he always, thought of as his *sorellina*, or kid sister.

Maria always had a passionate love of animals. Her circumstances would not permit her to have pets in her early years, but when she arrived in Venice she would adopt a stray dog who had wandered to the Palazzo for food. She named him "Boogie" after a popular song of the era. She would wash him in the bathtub at the Palazzo, and feed him. One day he became naughty and chewed or tore the fancy curtains covering the tall windows at the Palazzo. But Maria always protected "Boogie," the first dog that she would know and love, even from the house-keeping staff who took care of the rooms and furnishings.

Maria would grow to love Venice, and she became very familiar with all its famous treasures such as the Rialto Bridge, the Piazza San Marco, and the Grand Canal. She would ride the gondolas on the canal, and she and Louis had in reality a one year honeymoon that was never forgotten.

One by one the brothers began returning home to Blue Island from the war. The conflict in the Pacific finally ended, and Rosemary was able to see all her sons return safely. The five stars on the window on Cochran Street would come down as each brother came home. Henry, the youngest, whose departure for the war as the last brother to leave so upset Rosemary, was the first to arrive home. After seeing much combat Armand came home from the Philippines, and Maurice returned from France. Arthur never left the United States but served as a private at various stateside forts. Rosemary would fix her pasta specialities in the dining room on Cochran Street, and a decanter of wine and water was always on the table at every meal. The boys were still all single, and with the economy booming after the war they all were able to find jobs. Henry went to college at DePaul University and earned an accounting degree. Antoinette had matured into a young lady and had lived at home during the war, finishing school and beginning work.

The time for Louis and Maria in Venice would soon come to an end, as all good things in life have to end some time. In mid- to late-1946 Louis eventually made arrangements for Maria to leave for America, to go to Blue Island to live at the house with Rosemary, Antoinette and the brothers, while Louis continued his postwar military career. Louis would remain in Italy for several months more. Maria soon boarded a "liberty ship" for the long trip to America, a country she never dreamed of or planned to live in. She was what was called at the time a "war bride," not an immigrant like Antonio so many years before.

Later, after the Allied officers vacated the Palazzo, it was acquired in 1947 by American Peggy Guggenheim, who was born in 1898 and was heiress to the Guggenheim fortune. She was the daughter of Benjamin Guggenheim, who perished on the *Titanic*. Peggy would live there for many years with her notable art collection and her dogs, whom she loved like Maria. After Peggy died and was buried in the garden, the edifice was converted to an art museum under the auspices of the Guggenheim Foundation. It can be visited today, located at 701 Dorsoduro in Venice, and the exterior of the palace has changed little from when Maria and Louis lived there. The name of the palace translated from the Italian means "of the lions" (*dei leoni*) and although it is said that a lion was once kept in the garden, the more probably origin of the name is the fact that yawning lion heads in stone decorate the facade at the water's edge.

14

The Immediate Post-War Years

Louis would remain in Venice until January 7, 1947, when he would return to the United States, but remain in the army on active duty until March of 1947. On January 14, 1947, he was appointed a Captain in Military Intelligence. He also received on the same date an official appreciation letter from the War Department Adjutant General's Office, which confirmed his appointment in the Reserve Corps as an officer. He would serve in the Army Reserve until June of 1956, when he would receive his Honorable Discharge.

In November of 1945, just before he left Florence to go to Venice, Louis received an official commendation letter from Colonel John H. Harmony, Commanding the Army University Training Command. In it, he states that Louis provided "exemplary performance" of his assigned tasks. The letter to Louis states further: "Your diligence in the preparation of your subject matter, your constant efforts to present that material in an inspirational and effective manner, your care in evaluating and grading student attainment, and your constant willingness to advise and help your students—all have combined to help maintain a high level of scholastic achievement at the University Study Center. It is this very insistence upon the adequacy of material and the excellence of scholarship that has served to re-orient the thinking of military personnel and to prepare them for their return to the life and activities of civilian living." The letter concludes that Louis had discharged his duties with "excellence."

It is his setting, being a teacher in a military environment, so similar to his years at Culver, that Louis found so enjoyable and conducive to his training and interests. He was first and foremost a teacher and scholar, not a businessman. He would always be most happy in a classroom, teaching mature or adult students.

While Louis remained in Venice, Maria arrived in America, not going through Ellis Island, however, as Antonio and Rosemary had done. Maria would debark the liberty ship full of Italian war brides at a New York pier and be greeted by the Red Cross, which would help her connect with a train to Chicago. Maria had travelled with a number of Italian women on the boat, and she befriended one special person in particular, Sandra Colombo, who would settle in Herrin, Illinois, and would correspond with Maria for the rest of her life.

Maria's first exposure to America was the train trip to Chicago, where she was greeted by Arthur at the train station. From there she went to Cochran Street to meet Rosemary, Antoinette and the brothers. Maria still spoke little English, and she would never take a formal language course. She learned to speak fluent English entirely on her own. Always independent and self-sufficient, she would rapidly learn the ways of life in America, a land which she did not know except through the movies.

Rosemary welcomed her, and Maria soon adapted to living in Blue Island, and the lifestyle of the family. The brothers were working, and Maria would help with the laundry, ironing, and cleaning. As matriarch of the family Rosemary held sway in the kitchen, and the meals were her exclusive domain. At first Maria experienced an adjustment period, and one can only imagine the mixed emotions with which she faced this new life and new reality. The brothers and Antoinette were all uniformly kind to her, and she had a particular affection for Arthur, who was always very solicitous of her, and for Henry.

Maria would learn to go to the neighborhood grocery store, and do a number of errands. She meet "Boots," the dog owned by the Schilling family nearby, who became a mascot at the Cinabro home, scratching on the back porch door to come in and be fed. Rosemary became attached to "Boots," who was really another member of the family.

Soon Louis left Venice and returned to his home and family, the last brother to come back from Europe and the war. With a young wife new to the ways of America, and a crowded house, it was inevitable that Louis would seek to leave to start a new life and a new career. The post-war period for America was very prosperous, unlike the dark days of the Great Depression. Jobs and career opportunities were much more plentiful, and Louis soon answered a job notice in the newspaper advising of an opportunity at what was then the Upjohn Company at their world headquarters in Kalamazoo, Michigan. He travelled to Kalamazoo for the interview, and Maria also visited. Soon they learned that he had the job as a language translator in the International Division. Henry would recall how thrilled his brother was when he received the news, with Louis almost dancing with joy. This position offered more opportunity than did teaching, which in those days did not pay a living wage.

Maria was anxious to start her own home. Rosemary was a person of strong temperament and strict in her ways, and there was a generational as well as a cultural difference between Maria and Rosemary. Maria was from the north of Italy, and the Cinabros were of course from the south. Even to this day there are cultural and other differences which characterize the two sections of Italy. The history of each section is different, the dialects are vastly dissimilar, and the philosophy of life of each region is unique.

The matriarch Rosemary had overcome numerous economic and cultural obstacles to raise her six children and maintain the family homestead on Cochran Street in Blue Island after Tony had died. She had witnessed the country pass from the Great Depression through World War II, and had seen the family establish roots and finally begin to flourish in the new country. She had seen her five sons survive the war, when other families such as the Bowsers two doors down the street had lost their son valiantly fighting for his country. She always kept her strict "Old World" view of life and never relinquished her Southern Italian heritage. Family was everything to her.

In 1951 she developed liver disease. The beloved dog "Boots" was allowed in her sickroom, which gave her great joy. She stayed home on Cochran Street and Antoinette cared for her to the end. My only memory of Rosemary when I was about three years old is a faded image of seeing her in her sickbed with her arms raised, as she wanted to hold me. She passed away peacefully at home in 1951, and Louis and Maria and I returned from Kalamazoo to join the family for the funeral, and the burial next to Tony at Holy Sepulchre Cemetery. Antoinette, who had been devoted to her mother, had cared for her, and had lived at home, always remembered Rosemary's final words to her, "Take care of the family."

15

Antoinette

Taking care of the family Antoinette would certainly do. She would always live in and maintain the house on Cochran Street in Blue Island and give a home to Maurice and Arthur, who, like her, would never marry. She would assume the role of keeper of the hearth and of the family history. Sharing many of the characteristics of brother Louis, education would be central to her. She also shared his work ethic, patriotism, interest in current events and love of foreign languages.

Born in Naples, Italy, on January 2, 1916, (though her birthday is celebrated on December 30) with her given name of Maria Antoinette, she arrived at Ellis Island when the family returned from Italy in 1921 on the *Duca d' Aosta*. She graduated from Blue Island High School in June of 1933, at the height of the Great Depression, as class valedictorian. Her major was English, and she also studied Latin and French. She attended Morgan park Junior College, graduating in June of 1936 with a French-German-English major. After one year at the University of Chicago, with time off to work and to take care of the family, she received her B.A. degree from the University of Illinois at Champaign-Urbana in June of 1950. Despite the economic hardships of the Depression years, and the need to work during the war years after

Tony died, she reached her goal of completing her degree and certification as a teacher.

Also, like Louis, though teaching was her main forte, she would make her career in the corporate world, working for pharmaceutical giant, Abbott Laboratories, and later for the Continental Bank. Both she and Louis would have somewhat parallel careers in the pharmaceutical industry, while maintaining an interest in teaching and languages. They both loved literature and music, and were disciplined and hard working. They took great pride in their jobs.

As the only girl in the family she received a lot of attention from her father Tony, who used to make her hot cocoa in the basement of Cochran Street before the family could afford to put a kitchen on the upstairs floor. One has the feeling she was special to Tony, though he loved all his children. She would have been overjoyed had baby sister Filomena survived, and she may have suffered the most in the family when the baby died. She took loyal care of Rosemary in her later years.

Antoinette was nicknamed "Dorothy," for some unclear reason, but I call her Aunt "Junior," as the name Antoinette is the female derivative of her father's name. Of a generous and loving nature, she has a strong disposition and a total commitment to family. Maurice, who made a career with the postal service after he returned from his duty in France during the war, was the closest brother to her, and lived with her until he died in 1989. His unique sense of humor, and warm and engaging personality, always cheered her and brought a smile to her face. His death in 1989, at the age of seventy-three, was a great loss to her as it was, of course, to the rest of the family.

The force and resiliency of Antoinette was always a great source of support to me in my formative years, and especially the law school years. Though she and my father Louis would experience through the years a degree of sibling rivalry, their personalities were very similar and the love underneath was undeniable. She has supported every family activity and endeavor, and has been the symbol of the assimilation of the family that Tony founded in America into the American mainstream. Always proud to say she was born in Naples, her American patriotism and pride in her brothers' World War II service is always evident.

As I write this, dear Antoinette still thrives in Blue Island, and is the source of much of this family history. She is a unique and unforgettable person. She has been a fountain of strength to all in the family.

Antoinette, 1950

16

Kalamazoo Years

And so in 1947 Louis and Maria left Rosemary, Antoinette, and the brothers in the home in Blue Island and moved to Kalamazoo, Michigan, about 140 miles from the Chicago area, where they would settle and remain. Louis began his career at the Upjohn Company (now Pfizer), the pharmaceutical company which in those times had its world headquarters in Kalamazoo. They first rented an apartment on Walnut Street in downtown Kalamazoo. Maria would remember fondly those times as she continued to learn the ways of the strange new world.

Soon they bought a house, the only house Maria would ever call her own, at 1104 Royce Avenue in the Midwood section of town, which was annexed to the city in the early 1950s. There they would remain, raising me and making an immaculate and loving home which Maria forever became attached to.

Louis was a language translator and, like Antoinette, he took great pride in his work. The Upjohn company marketed many of their products in Europe and Latin America, calling for translation of letters and label copy and scientific documents. He would remain for twenty-five years, retiring in 1972. He produced a paper called "The Art of Translating" which reflected his mastery of the English language and literary background. In it he states in part, "A translation, being a creative work, is something new, apart from the thing translated. It is the production of an individuality. For this reason, there are as many translations as there are translators. For example, a letter given to translate into another language to twelve different people may very well result in twelve different translations all of which may be correct but no two of which may be alike in style and phraseology. Once again, the creative ability of the translator comes into play. It is the business of the Upjohn International Translation Department to supply honest and accurate translations. The work is difficult except for the routine pieces. The legal, commercial, promotional and scientific material involved is the basis for production and sales. It is our conviction that this special department is doing a capital job and that it is always eager to meet new challenges, as Upjohn International grows and grows."

His love of foreign languages extended to tutoring many students over the years, in high school, college, and as adults. He felt most comfortable in the classroom, and his tutoring gave him an outlet for his passion for teaching others. He would continue his prodigious reading and the house was filled with the classics in English, Spanish, French and Italian.

His love of literature led him to write a number of book reviews for such national publications as *Books Abroad* and the University of Oklahoma Press. He would correspond with many people, such as Warner Williams from the Culver years, and many comrades from the war years. A special friend was lawyer Isabel Jacobs, whom he met as a student at the University of Chicago, and they would stay in touch and visit for the rest of their lives. His brother Maurice and he would carry on an active correspondence until Maurice died in 1989.

Perhaps Louis would have been most happy teaching

at the Culver Military Academy, or at some college campus, but the Upjohn Company gave him the security of working for a major international corporation. He would rise early in the morning to take the company bus to work, Kalamazoo in those days being very much a "company town" (much more so than today). Always gregarious by nature, more so than Maria, he made many friends at the company and elsewhere.

He continued serving in the Army Reserve until 1956. The Korean War came but he did not have to serve overseas. During the McCarthy Era and the Korean War, he would attend Army Reserve meetings, and he continued wearing his army jacket until well into the 1970s. The army life was something he never forgot, and he always looked back at those exciting days with nostalgia and fondness.

Louis was a good provider and always saved money, the Depression years never far from his memory. Maria was a homemaker, in an era when most mothers stayed home and raised their families, and two income households were a rarity. She nurtured me and took excellent care of me. The fact that she did not have a mother when she was raised was always part of her consciousness.

During the post-war years the children of Tony and Rosemary made successful lives. Armand, the war hero, married Florence Cianci and raised Billy and David. He would go on to a long and successful career at the Ford Motor Company in Chicago. Henry graduated from college after the war and married Berniece Allie. They met while they both worked for the Santa Fe Railroad. Together they lived in Blue Island and raised Stephen, Mark and Timothy. "Hank" went on to a rewarding career with the American Library Association in Chicago. Antoinette and Maurice, who continued living on Cochran

Street in the family homestead along with Arthur, worked hard at their careers and retired to enjoy their years living in the house so full of memories. Tony did not live to see it, but his children had successfully assimilated into the American mainstream. Hard work, discipline, education, and pride in America were instilled in all the children, and the poor but dignified man who came through Ellis Island would have been proud.

The memories of his years in Blue Island and with the family never left Louis. I remember many weekends and Thanksgivings as a young boy making the five-hour Greyhound bus trip with my father from Kalamazoo to Chicago on old Highway U.S. 12, arriving in Blue Island at the family homestead for a warm pasta meal prepared by Rosemary, and then later by Antoinette. Often he would bring back to Kalamazoo boxes and suitcases full of books, riding on the bus and making friends with the passengers, many of whom he would communicate with later. He always loved his home in Blue Island. Maria would join us for some, but not all, of these trips.

Travel was a large part of my upbringing during the Kalamazoo years of my parents, and even though my family did not have a car until I turned nineteen years of age, after my freshman year in college, Louis and Maria provided me with an opportunity to see many places. Maria felt the need to return to her native Mantua and her family, and beginning in 1952 she made the first of her five trips to Europe, staying at the home of brother Nando and his wife Iris, and greeting their children Daniela and Angelo. My first memory is of my parents and me waiting at the train station in Kalamazoo on one foggy morning, and seeing the old New York Central train arrive out of the mist to take me and my mother to

New York City, to board a boat in 1952 for the ten day trip to Italy.

Of the five trips Maria would make across the Atlantic, I accompanied her on three, in 1952, 1958, and in 1963, travelling on the last trip on the *Queen Elizabeth* and returning on the *Queen Mary* of the Cunard Line. The first trip was aboard old Italian ships called the *Vulcania* and *Saturnia.* In 1958 we flew TWA. These voyages were unforgettable, as were the times in Italy in Mantua and Rome, visiting Maria's family. Maria flew to Italy alone on her last two trips, in 1967, and 1969, my college studies preventing me from traveling with her. Maria was in Italy in the summer of 1969 and watched from there on television with the world and Nando and his family, as Neil Armstrong became the first man on the moon, fulfilling President Kennedy's goal.

Uncle Nando (Zio Nando in Italian) Brevigilieri and his loving wife Iris made our stays warm and enjoyable, and Maria would finally be able to enjoy life without worrying about the necessities of survival. I have nothing but warm and affectionate feelings for those long ago days in Italy, and of the dear and kind people of Maria's family, including sister Teresa Braghini and her husband Francesco, and brother Stelio Breviglieri and his wife Julianna, who lived in the Venice area, the scene of such happiness for Louis and Maria in that first year after the war. Another special person was Aunt Ginia, the strong and kind person who helped raise Maria, and who I was fortunate to meet along with her daughter Gianna. Maria would correspond with her Italian relatives all her life, and when the satellites made phone calls to Europe a convenient experience, she would enjoy calling them by telephone from Kalamazoo.

Maria never forgot for one minute of her life her

Northern Italian heritage. She was always most proud of it, and of the ancient culture which produced her values and philosophy of the world. On November 17, 1953, in Kalamazoo County Circuit Court, Maria became a naturalized United States citizen, and, as Tony and Rosemary before her, she embraced her new country. She would eventually live more than twice as many years in America as in Italy, but still her European ways would always be a part of her. Certain elements of American culture she would always have difficulty adjusting to, but for the most part she became a part of the life and culture of Kalamazoo.

In the 1960s she would work part-time outside of the home, at Western Michigan University in the registrar's office during student registration, and she enjoyed being around the students. She learned English, like Tony, through self-education, and she became a voracious reader of the newspaper and books in English. Sharing with Louis a love of literature and music, the house would be filled on Saturday mornings with the sound of Italian opera records playing from the phonograph, in the days long before CDs and cassettes. Italian chamber music records from composers such as Vivaldi were also favorites of Louis. Though a private person and less socially gregarious than Louis, Maria would enjoy working for the United Nations Society in Kalamazoo. She was always curious about foreign cultures and societies. She detested chauvinism and provincialism, and she had a very tolerant view of other customs and religions.

And so while Louis, like his father Tony, served as the "breadwinner" of the family, Maria, as her mother-in-law Rosemary before her, tended to the hearth and home. Louis retired from Upjohn in 1972, and lived another eighteen years at home on Royce Avenue. He forever maintained his reading and writing passion, and his letters and book reviews continued to occupy his hours. In April of 1962 he wrote to the Viking Press in New York about a mistake he caught in a book called *My Brother's Keeper,* by Stanislaus Joyce (The Viking Press, New York, 1958). To illustrate his knowledge of literature and the breadth of his capacities the following is quoted from that letter: "Stanislaus Joyce states, 'At Trieste we went to see *Il Cantico dei Cantici* by Giacosa' (page 258). A footnote is given about Giacosa on same page . . . Giacosa *never* wrote such a play. The author of *Il Cantico dei Cantici* was Felice Cavaliotti (1842–1898). He was a mediocre poet and a writer of romantic plays of little value. . . . On the other hand, Giuseppe Giacosa was a fine dramatist and an excellent librettist."

If Louis could have written books and plays, while teaching languages, he would have fulfilled his dreams. He was never a "businessman" in the traditional sense, even though he worked in the corporate world. Because he had to face so much adversity during his formative years, and because of the intervening world war, with the notable exception of the Culver years, much of his academic talent and knowledge probably went underappreciated by most, except those of us who knew him and loved him.

He loved to meet people of every walk of life, and to discuss the events of the world. I remember countless people coming to the house, and many trips to visit friends and acquaintances. Time does not permit in this account the listing of all the friends he would visit or write letters to. His contacts were diverse and numerous, and not necessarily always from the academic world. To illustrate, a good friend was a professor at Western Michigan University in Kalamazoo, Ruth Van Horn, who loved to come to the house to discuss with Louis literature and the arts. Another friend from Chicago days was Joe Savoldi, an Associated Press Second Team All-American football player from Notre Dame, who played for the great Knute Rockne. Savoldi, a famous name in the late twenties and early thirties, still holds a Notre Dame stadium record for kickoff return and lived in Three Oaks, Michigan. I still treasure a picture of the great Savoldi holding me in his arms when I was a small child during one of our visits to see him. From that day the mystique of Notre Dame football became part of me.

Travel was so much of my life growing up that boats and trains and plains were an indelible part of my youth. For three summers in a row in the 50s the three of us would take the New York Central "Wolverine" across Canada to New York City, to spend two weeks in Manhattan and the Bronx visiting army friends such as Claude Bove and Louis Conte and their families. Long dinners with pasta and wine and friends in New York City during those mellow summer nights, and driving to the piers of New York City to look at the docked ocean liners, are fondly remembered.

After retirement Louis did not travel as much, and his health began to decline. Finally he had to put aside his beloved books, and his world gradually melted into his home, with Maria caring for him lovingly. He died peacefully at home in Kalamazoo on October 9, 1990, having lived to see me marry Pamela in 1972. Before he died he lived to see the arrival of his grandchildren, Jennifer and Michael, and they were a source of joy even as he became somewhat incapacitated. Maria, always the faithful wife and supporter, would be with him to the last. She grieved deeply for him, and even though they had been through so much together during the war years, she suffered over his loss as she had not before. He was brought back to Chicago, to Holy Sepulchre Cemetery, to be laid to rest near his brothers Maurice and Arthur, and not far from the graves of Tony and Rosemary.

In time Maria would adjust to her life alone. She remained forever at the Royce Avenue home, and it became her source of pride and joy. Her love of animals kept her busy feeding and caring for her beloved backyard birds and squirrels, probably the best fed in Kalamazoo! She loved the family dogs "Lupo," "Misty," and "Sierra," treating them as children, and giving countless hours to their care when we were absent. In her late years she became somewhat reclusive. Always a private person, and enjoyed her solitude after a life of so much turmoil and upheaval.

Her privacy did not deter her interest in history and current events. She followed the news with great curiosity, and witnessed the terrible events of September 11, 2001, ushering in a new war, and she was deeply affected by it. She would read the local newspaper from cover to cover. She enjoyed taking trips with me and Michael, and was able to see the Grand Canyon in a raft, and ride a horse at the age of seventy two in Colorado. The love of travel never waned until her health declined. She saw Jennifer graduate from high school and Michael develop into a young man.

Over the years she had developed a special fondness for her niece, Daniela Breviglieri, the daughter of brother Nando. Daniela, who married Livio Vicari, lived in Mantua and would correspond with Maria faithfully over the years, and talk frequently by telephone in later years. When Daniela and husband Livio came to America in November of 2000 for the New York Marathon, in which they participated, they made a special trip to Kalamazoo to visit Maria. Maria's health had begun to decline, but we had a special day to be remembered as Daniela and Livio were shown Kalamazoo and the house on Royce Avenue, the home which Maria so painstakingly and lovingly made her refuse and "castle."

Another special person in Maria's life, who became closer to her as the years went by, was Cheryl TenBrink (nee Whitman). The girl who grew up across the street on Royce Avenue, and who was and is a special friend to me, became almost like a daughter to Maria, who used to love to show Cheryl her yard and garden and house. Cheryl and husband Burton helped Maria greatly in her last days, as she struggled with failing health.

It is still too painful for me to recount in detail the passing of my mother. At the age of eighty she died very bravely and with a very calm and philosophical demeanor on May 3, 2002. Her ashes were taken to Chicago, where they lie next to her beloved Louis, in Holy Sepulchre Cemetery. She had told me she had not wanted to be taken to Italy. She was, in the final analysis, an American, and she would not leave the man who had ushered her into the New World. Tony never met his daughter-in-law, and she did not come through Ellis Island as he did. But even though both returned to Italy, they never wavered in their love for their adopted country.

Maria always said her life seemed like a dream. She was a unique person with a vivacious and loving personality, and I can never forget her. Ironically, just a few days after her death, her beloved Aunt Ginia, the strong spirited woman who had raised Maria in Italy, and who had lived a long and fulfilling life, died in Salsomaggiore, the placid resort town in Italy where she lived with her daughter Gianna. She had shared with Maria a strong and independent nature, and a special courage in facing life. She was a central part of Maria's life, and even though they were separated by years and distance, death brought them together within days.

All mothers are special. My mother was special to me. Maria never asked for, nor received, much from life that was not earned, endured or worked for. She endured growing up without a mother, escaping from death in the German occupation of Rome, and coming to a strange new world, after marrying the man who had travelled across the ocean in the army to meet her. She would cross the Atlantic Ocean eleven times. She possessed a zest for life that matched that of Tony's son Louis, her beloved husband. She could be happy with the smallest thing, and a butterfly or a firefly in her backyard could give her joy. Like Tony, the father-in-law she would never know, she was a survivor and a strong citizen of the New World of America. With the dignity of Tony, she never had regrets, and was brave to the last.

17

Random Thoughts

And so why have I written this, and what have I accomplished? I hoped for a record of these people, whose lives otherwise were at risk of being forever forgotten in the mists of time. Hopefully, a hundred years from now, someone descended from me and Pam will read this, and learn about these people, and ask questions, and know them a little bit. I will have accomplished something if this happens. I hope my children, Jennifer and Michael, will encourage their children and grandchildren to read it.

Have I captured these people, who have left us with memories, and some writings, and some pictures? Probably only a tiny bit. There is so much more that can be recounted, and I hope others will take an interest. There are so many more people I could have mentioned, whose names do not appear here. I love history, and I thought it would be useful for this to be a start to a family history, whose chapters can continue to be written. I hope this has been a small glimpse, like looking through a keyhole, through time, so a part of our history is not forgotten.

What follows are some thoughts and observations, in no particular order. My parents, Louis and Maria, were not perfect. They were all too human, and were never afraid to admit it. But they lived by a philosophy that was found on a piece of paper I found in my Dad's materials. It was apparently given to him by his good friend from his Culver days, Warner Williams, the art professor and sculptor who had the Geodesic Dome Studio in Culver, Indiana. It reads: "There will be only one of you in all of time. That identity is cancelled if you are not always fearlessly yourself." Louis and Maria were never afraid to be themselves. They were each fiercely individualistic, and did not believe in being "conformists." They both had more than their share of suffering, and war, and economic deprivation, but they never felt sorry for themselves, they lived life to the fullest, and had a curiosity about all things.

Aside from my parents, a person I drew closer to while preparing this was Antonio, (Tony), the grandfather I never knew, who came through Ellis Island that cold day one hundred years ago. His quiet courage resonated as I researched his life and times. I still cannot comprehend that he never enjoyed a vacation, never drove a car, and never stopped working until he died. And yet he persevered, and survived, and became an American after all. What comes through time is his dignity, and sense of pride, and quiet patriotism.

The values and experiences illustrated by the lives of most of the people recounted in this story are summarized as follows. First, my parents, grandparents on both sides, and my uncles and aunts, believed in a work ethic. Hard work and perseverance were the hallmarks of their lives. They did not have a sense of entitlement, or expectation. They did not believe the world owed them a living. They worked, and they did not question or whine or complain.

Secondly, education was a central part of their lives, whether as in the case of Louis or Antoinette or Henry it was a formal college education, or as in the case of Antonio and Maria, their education came through learning a new language on their own, or learning a trade, or travelling the world. The value of and respect for education was always key. Maria's long lost mother, Ermetina, was one of the few university educated women of her era in Italy.

They were a law-abiding and disciplined lot, the Cinabros, and so was Maria. Living life by the rules, being clean and neat, and organized, was a focus of their lives. I cannot think of anyone more organized, and neat, than my late mother, who kept her home on Royce Avenue so immaculate.

They all shared, at some point in their lives, economic deprivation. Isabel Jacobs, the good and dear college friend from University of Chicago days of my father Louis, once told my mother, "They were so poor, Maria, they were poor . . ." referring to the Cinabros during the dark Depression years. There were no "silver spoons" given to my family. Everything obtained was earned through hard work.

Patriotism in a quiet, unassuming way, was a trademark. Tony fought for Italy in World War I, the five brothers fought for America after Pearl Harbor, and Maria loved both her old country in Italy and her new land in America. She always said the *patria* was important, and worth defending. She believed in respect for government, and greatly admired the democratic system in the United States which she could compare knowingly to other systems.

My mother used to say "The more you have, the unhappier you will be." She never believed in material wealth or conspicuous consumption. She loved simplicity, order, and respect for others. I am grateful I was her son.